LIVING IN SPITE OF
CEREBRAL PALSY

LIVING IN SPITE OF CEREBRAL PALSY

Miss Donna Hughes

authorHOUSE®

AuthorHouse™ UK Ltd.
1663 Liberty Drive
Bloomington, IN 47403 USA
www.authorhouse.co.uk
Phone: 0800.197.4150

© 2014 Miss Donna Hughes. All rights reserved.

No part of this book may be reproduced, stored in a retrieval system, or transmitted by any means without the written permission of the author.

Published by AuthorHouse 05/15/2014

ISBN: 978-1-4969-7956-8 (sc)
ISBN: 978-1-4969-7957-5 (e)

Library of Congress Conrol Number: 2014909277

Any people depicted in stock imagery provided by Thinkstock are models, and such images are being used for illustrative purposes only. Certain stock imagery © Thinkstock.

Because of the dynamic nature of the Internet, any web addresses or links contained in this book may have changed since publication and may no longer be valid. The views expressed in this work are solely those of the author and do not necessarily reflect the views of the publisher, and the publisher hereby disclaims any responsibility for them.

CHAPTER ONE

HOW MY LIFE BEGAN

My life began on June the 2nd 1963 I was born in a hospital called Buckland in Dover in Kent England. There were some complications at my birth the cord was wrapped around my neck and my brain was starved of oxygen and that meant as I was growing up my speech wouldn't be normal, I would not be able to walk and my hands would not work properly. I was lying across my mum's tummy instead of downwards and my right arm was behind my back, my feet came out first and one foot came out before the other. First of all the doctors told my mum that they didn't think I would last the night out but I proved them all wrong as you can see, then the doctors told my mum I would grow up as a cabbage not being able to do anything, but yet again I proved them wrong. My disability is called Cerebral Palsy, which means a part of my brain is damaged the part which controls my muscles, and my speech and I can't walk at all I have been in a wheel chair all of my life. When I was three years old I had to go into hospital to have a couple of teeth out, and it ended up they took all my teeth out, and they said that I wouldn't get any more teeth the rest of my life, but thank god my teeth did grow back, but while I was waiting for my other teeth to grow I was given the nickname of Mrs. Gumage, I found that quite funny myself.

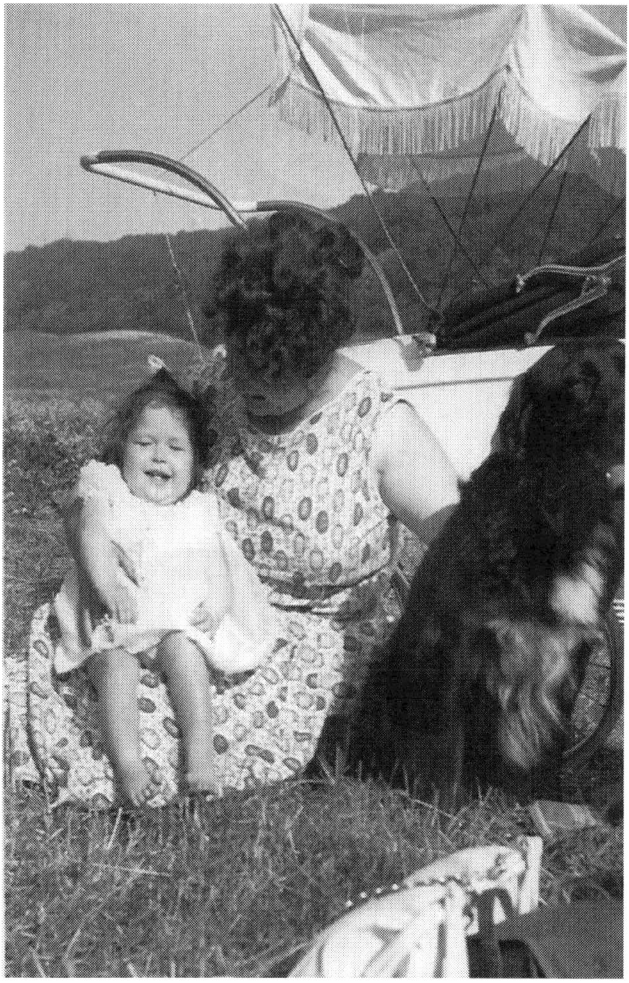

I can remember going shopping with my mum and my Nan, other children would point, stare and laugh at me because I looked different I suppose, I would get so angry, but if I was out with my sisters they would always stick up for me, by saying "what you looking at," or "do you want a picture," my sister Lyn would say that, that would make me laugh. I can remember when my sister Lyn would push me in my wheelchair, if anyone was in her way she would just push my wheelchair into their legs, she would always say, "can't you see I'm pushing my sister in a wheelchair?" She was so funny my sister Lyn. I was and I still am very proud of my two sisters I've got two beautiful sisters, they are called Diane and Lyn and I've got a brother called Colin who I am very proud of too, Diane is five years older than me, Lyn is four years older than me, Colin is three years older than me, as I was growing up I never felt any different from my sisters or my brother because they all treated me normally. Every morning before school my sisters and my brother would all take turns to hold me and help me to walk, if it was a nice morning they would walk me around the garden by holding me under my arms. I can also remember going shopping with mum and her friend Silvia and her son Harry, we went to Folkestone in Kent we went by train, mum would always buy me a toy, I never ever went without when I was a little girl thanks to my mum, I still don't go without now. Before I had a wheelchair I had this blue and white buggy, and then my very first wheelchair was blue, in those days I always used to stick stickers on each side of my wheelchairs, the stickers I would put on my wheelchair would be of my favorite pop stars, with every wheelchair that I have had I have broken the foot rests because I have to push on them to sit myself up, but as I always say I keep the wheelchair man in a job. What I can remember of my birth father he didn't do anything for me as a dad, thinking back now he never gave me cuddles or kisses, my mum did and she still does, my birth father left my mum when I was still at school, he left mum for one of her friend's that mum used to worked with, some friend huh. When my birth father left I used to go to his house for Sunday dinner, and when I got older and I starting saying to myself, here why am I sitting round here because I was getting older to realize what he had done to my mum, so one evening I phoned him up and I said look I want to see you dad but without her the woman who he left my mum for and he said to me, no you see both of us or you don't see me, I said fine disown me then and I haven't heard from him since and I never want to.

I started my school days a bit late in my life I was eight years old when I started school because they couldn't find a school suitable for me, but then they found a school called Langhorne in Broadstairs Kent, which was just for disabled children, we were living in Dover at the time I had to get to Sandwich to get a taxi to take me to Broadstairs, I used to have an escort to travel there and back with, I remember when I had to leave my mum I used to scream my head off every day but by the time I got to school I was alright. At school they taught me to read, until this very day I can remember the books I read every day, they were called Peter and Jane, and we also did math's, that was my worst subject I was so useless at math's, and I still am even now, we used to do some coloring in I wasn't so good at that because I would go over the lines. I tried to write but my hand writing would always come out scruffy and big. I remember when we were in the classroom we used to keep our work in a tray and I used to like to keep my tray tidy, I used to take all my work out of my tray and put it back all neat and tidy for some reason I enjoyed doing that. In the mornings we used do our work and then half way through the morning we would have break time and we were always given a cup of milk and I looked forward to break times just to get a cup of milk. When it was play time there was this three wheeler bike which I loved riding, they would strap me on it and strap my feet to the pedal's so that they wouldn't slip off and the bike had a special belt that held me and the other children who used to sit on it, I was riding on the bike one play time quite happily and then all of a sudden I went over the handle bars, the teachers wouldn't let me ride it anymore after that. I had a very, very, very special friend at Lanthorne school, Susie Prior she was so sweet, her disability was worse than mine, she could only communicate with her eyes, she couldn't walk or talk at all, but she knew what you were saying, I remember I used to try to feed her sometimes, what a laugh we would have, we used to go to each other's birthday parties, I remember Susie had a crush on my brother Colin, as soon as she would see him her pretty little face would light up like a Christmas tree also she would get the giggles, sadly Susie died a few years ago, I felt so angry how could they take someone as beautiful as Susie away from this world.

When I was a young girl and at my first school I had this doll called Thumberlina she had a cord in her back that you pulled and she would wiggle when she laid on the floor, she wore a yellow baby grow I used to take her everywhere with me I even took her to school, my first school Lanthorne I even had my school photo taken holding her, yes I know I'm a sad person but she was such a cute doll, but then one day something awful happened one morning my mum was carrying me down stairs in those days I was a light weight, as mum was carrying me down stairs I dropped Thumberlina I was really upset my mum tried to fix her, but she couldn't Thumberlina was my favourite doll.

When I was at Lanthorne School I had physiotherapy, which was to keep my muscle's strong, I used to have to lay on the floor and they would stretch my arms and legs, and I would have to sit on the floor crossed legged and I had to sit up straight on my own, and then they walked me between two people I used to enjoy walking with two people it felt so good, I tried to walk with a walker but I wasn't very good at that there was this special standing box, which they would stand me in it for about half an hour so that my legs could get strong. When I did exercises I was using all my muscles in my body, which was good for me, also I had to walk between some bars holding on to each side I did that quite well.

At first I didn't like any of the teachers at Lanthorne, but then this very special teacher came along Miss Bell was her name before she got married, and then she became Mrs. Saunders I became very close to her, she used to call me her sunshine, she would always take time to explain things to me the other teachers were never like that, I will always remember I wouldn't eat the dinners at school, so Mrs. Saunders told me to tell my mum to do a packed lunch up every day and Mrs. Saunders said that I could eat my lunch with her so that's what I did, I remember mum used to pack me up with little sausages' on sticks and sandwich's, and some fruit with some other stuff, I can still remember Mrs. Saunders said little sausages were her favorites, so every day I used to save one just for her, I think she liked that. The thing I enjoyed most about Mrs. Saunders was that she made me feel special, although I know that I'm not any different from any other person who has a disability, Mrs. Saunders used to wheel me out of the class room when it was home time each day and she would please me by placing her hands on my shoulders, and this would make me feel so very special, some people might have intimated that I was the teacher's pet, but because she was so good with me I didn't care. Every day after we had our school dinner we used to have to go for a rest and we had to lay down on these little camp beds for about half an hour or so, but I could never get to sleep in the day, I used to lay there chatting to my friend Susie, and then when we went back to the classroom we would watch telly, we would watch a programme called Watch with Mother but that was when I first started at Lanthorne, the programmes were called the Wooden Tops, Andy Pandy, Trumpton and some other programmes. We would watch those programmes every afternoon and then get back to our work. When I was at Lanthorne I had to have speech therapy because my speech was pretty bad. I also had three other close friends at Lanthorne and they were Chris Kirby, Donna Cripps and Collette Pearlman we were all very close. We used to have sports day every summer and we used to have wheel chair races and egg and spoon races, which were great fun and enjoyed by all participants, I got mum to take my photo with Mrs. Saunders and Pat, at our Christmas party, and I just admired her teaching and understanding of my problems so very, very, much. At Lanthorne School they had a heated swimming pool and that was great fun even though I had to do exercise's, I always enjoyed swimming the pool was so big and what I liked was that they only had a few children in at one time, I got used to swimming on my front and on my back, but I needed someone to hold me though. There was one year I got stuck at school because it was snowing and they couldn't get us back to Dover, next door to my school there was a home for the mentally handicapped and me and another girl Dawn Streeter had to stay at Lanthorne House, which was awful I did not like it at all, at that time I had never been away from my mum before, I had to stay there only for one night, but it felt like years, there were a lot of mentally handicapped children who lived there and it felt quite scary.

Every Christmas at Lanthorne School we used to have a Christmas party and Father Christmas used to come and hand out presents, we sang some carols all of our parents came to watch, Mrs. Saunders used to play both piano and the guitar, separately of course, after we sang some carols we would sit down for some food.

There were trained nurses at Lanthorne school to take the children like me to the toilet and help us at lunch time, and I can remember this one nurse, Nurse Mac was her name her real name was Joan, but at school I knew her as Nurse Mac she was such a good nurse, she would invite me round her house for weekends, she lived in Broadstairs and when I went to Joan's house I met her husband Reg and her daughter Ann, I used to stay for weekends that was cool that was, I made good friends with Ann as well.

When I went to my secondary school I found it hard at times, not the work it was the other kids as they would take the Mickey out of me on the way I spoke, my other friends who were disabled were alright because their speech was normal and clear, I had a couple of able bodied friends. I fancied this one boy at my school Dave Rider he was really nice, I can remember writing him a little note telling him how I felt, and he wrote me a little note back, we got I\n touch again a few years ago on the Internet and started chatting to each other, until I went and ruined it by showing my feelings for him and now we don't talk to each other at all. In my life I haven't been lucky in love, maybe I am meant to be single because of the way I am.

In the 70s there was this puppet show on the telly called Sooty and Sweep they were hand puppets, I was only eight or nine at the time and one day they came to our school Lanthorne, I had my picture taken with Harry Corbett, the man who used to do the show and Sooty. When I was young and at Lanthorne school I got my sister Lyn to colour my fringe and it went ginger it was meant to go blonde and I got told off by this nurse she said I was too young.

Then there came a sad day when I had to leave Lanthorne School and go to an able bodied school that was a very, very sad day for me having to leave Mrs. Saunders. I can remember the day I left, Mrs. Saunders and Pat who was a helper they were both waving me off on my last day there and I cried and cried, I asked Mrs. Saunders if we could keep in touch and she said yes. I started corresponding with her and was even invited to her family home after she had her baby son Matthew, Pat was kind enough to take me to see my teacher friend and I am still in touch with this very kind lady to this very day. {God bless her}

The able bodied school I attended was a secondary modern school called Conyngham, which was situated in Ramgate I started there in about 1975. I was fortunate enough to be there with my three special friends from my previous school, we all became prefects we used to have to be on lift duty to make sure the other kids didn't mess around in them. There was a helper there, Mrs. Luck we all disliked her very much and I had good reason to do so because I really wanted to sit my English exam she told me that I wouldn't be able to manage it, anyway they finally relented and let me sit the exam, I had to go into a small room on my own I had to have someone to write for me, and guess who I got helping me? Yes Mrs Luck, but anyway I got through it and I managed to pass at grade

5, I know it's not that great but at least I can say I tried even with Mrs Luck. I also tried to do some driving lesson's, but that was a big no, no I nearly backed into a teachers car, so they advised me not to drive. I stayed at that school until the sixth year although I didn't want to, but there wasn't anywhere else for me to go, until they found a College in Lancaster.

I can remember when I started my secondary school I had to start wearing glasses and I used to hate wearing them, I used to think to myself another disability, so I wouldn't wear them, but these days I have to wear them all of the time I can't do without them, when I was young I used to worry about my looks for god knows why, I remember hiding my glasses in my school bag, I also took my own lunch when I went to my secondary school I used to have to sit outside Mrs Luck's office in case I needed any help.

When I was about to leave my secondary school I really wanted to be a typist, but they said I was too slow I really enjoy typing it's something that I can do by myself, and with typing I have achieved so much in my life. There are something's I regret doing and saying in my life sometimes I say things without thinking and it lands me in trouble, I can be a nasty person at times and I'm not proud of that at all.

I went to College in 1981 for a year; it was called Beaumont College, which was just for young disabled students, being far away meant I had to live there, but came home for holidays. I got on alright there, I had to do a lot for myself, like dressing, washing, cooking and we had other lectures like typing, drama, my favorite lecture was typing. I was 17 coming up 18 when I was at College, I made a lot of friends there my best friend was Sarah, we used to travel together, we had to get a train from Euston train station to Lancaster train station, we became good friends. I had another good friend at College Leslie was her name, we always used to hang out together, there was a hall next to our College and we used to have disco's there and Leslie and I would dance around in our wheelchairs. I even had a few boyfriends, three, to be honest! There was Graham, Chris and John, but Graham was my main one; Graham and I used to go out for meals, and we would even go shopping together, we went to Blackpool some weekends, which was fun. When the carers took us to Blackpool Graham and I went on the ghost train I used to like that because we would cuddle up together, we went on tram rides in Blackpool too. Only doing a year at College I really regret because I could have done two years, but I admit I was missing home and my mum and dad, my step dad that is, my birth father I couldn't give a dam about him, my step dad was more of a father to me than my birth father ever was. When I became 18 I change my surname from Grant to Hughes because my mum got re-married the year before, but I had to wait until I was 18, so as soon as I was, I changed it straight away I didn't want to be known as a Grant anymore.

When I came home from College mum and dad took me back up there for a weekend so that I could see my boy/friend Graham and all my other friends. Graham and I were kissing that much that weekend that I ended up with Braced lips, when mum saw me she thought that Graham had smacked me in the mouth, but we were just making up for lost time. Graham and I used to send messages to each other on cassettes through the mail when I left College because it was easier for Graham because he found it hard to write down what he was thinking, I used to keep every single cassette with Grahams messages on and I played them over and over, between our messages on the cassettes we would play some of our favourite music, I used to look forward to getting Graham's cassettes through the post and listening to them in my bedroom, I never recorded over any of Graham's messages, but I think he did mine yet I didn't mind, but as time went by we stopped getting in touch with each other, which is a shame really because Graham was my first real love and he will always live in my memory.

After I came home from College I stayed at home for a while and then they found me a place in a day centre called Victoria House, which was in Westbrook near Margate Kent. First of all I went twice a week and then I went three times a week. I found it quite boring until they got this man in to teach computers, Dave was his name; but he wasn't there for long I can't remember why Dave left. This lady called Jill and this man called Arthur they were neighbours', and they both came to help with lunch times, I became good friends with Jill. Jill would always nag me about not eating my lunch, not nastily. Whenever there were trips on Jill would always push me, Jill took me on a boat trip to France on our own that was great fun, Jill also took me to the pictures to see a couple of films. The films she took me to see were Rainman, she also took me to see the film called The Twins, and we also went to London Zoo, and Jill brought her grandson Clarke with her, he had a condition with his lungs and sadly he died bless him. He was so young, he left me some Garfield books in his will because he knew I was a Garfield fan, I thought that was so sweet of him, and he even wrote me a letter with the books saying that he wanted me to have his books, I cried my eyes out when I read his letter. Not long after Clarke died Jill moved up to Scotland and I was so upset because Jill meant so much to me and she still does, we still write to each other we were and we still are and we will always be very close friends, before Jill went to Scotland she came to see me and she brought me this beanie teddy bear, which I take to bed with me every night, I know some people might think that I maybe a big kid, but Jill means a lot to me and when I hold onto that bear every night I hold onto our friendship.

I went to Victoria House by ambulance, I became very fond of a driver his name was Peter. I remember Peter came and took me out in his car one day we went for a coffee, which was nice. I met a girl called Wendy at Victoria House she was in a wheel chair like me we became good friends, we went on disabled holidays together and we had great fun, it was a holiday camp at Hayling Island in Portsmouth and for a week they had helpers there the group were called The Kent Association For The Disabled, when I first started going it was twice a year, May and September, there were some good helpers they treated you great, I remember these two male helpers when I first started going to camp they were called Dave and Barry I liked them both so much. I started going to camp in 1979 it was such great fun, they had live entertainment every night, there was even a bar there selling alcoholic drinks. I was 16 when I started going, but I had to miss a year when I went to college, but when I came back from college I started going to camp again, and met this married couple called Brenda and Eddie. Brenda used to look after me every year from the first year I met her. I became good friends with Eddie and Brenda, they even asked me to stay at their house now and then, and what a laugh that was. When I was staying with them every morning Eddie would wake me up playing his banjo, Eddie is a big fan of George Formby. Eddie and Brenda have got a daughter called Karen and she became a helper at camp. Karen and I also became friends, I had a great time there; sadly again a few years ago Brenda fell ill and passed away that was such a shock, Brenda was such a lovely and kind person. I don't hear from Eddie anymore, which is a shame.

When I went to camp in 1986 I met this guy called Les. He kept giving me the old eye, he was disabled himself, but he could walk. Anyway, we started to get to know each other well; we met in the May 1986 and got engaged in the October. I can even remember the date and day, it was on Monday the 6th of October and we got engaged by the sea, he brought an engagement ring with a wedding ring to go with it. Anyway, everything was rosy for a while he even came to meet my mum and dad. I knew that they did not like him at all by the way they acted. He came from Leytonstone in East London, when we were apart from each other we would write letters to each other. Les used to write loads of beautiful letters to me and I kept every single one of them, things were going great and then things started to go wrong. My friend Wendy wrote me a letter telling me that Les was cheating on me and I was heartbroken, like all men he denied it, so after that I split up with him. I kept my engagement ring though, but in temper I ripped all of his letters up, which I regret doing now because they would have been nice to keep, but at the time I was so hurt and upset.

There was another helper I made friends with Rob Hunt, we were such good friends as well, but as years went by I lost touch with Rob, we didn't fall out we just lost contact with each other. At camp there was a swimming pool and I used to go in with Rob, once he put my legs around his neck and dragged me around the pool I was safe as I had a rubber ring on. Also in the evenings when there were bands or \a disco's on Rob would lift me out of my chair and hold me in his arms and dance with me that would make my night, Rob was the only helper who would lift me out of my chair, he was great!

There was one time I went to camp and Eddie and Barry put me in my wheelchair on a table and walked off and left me but it was a joke they made me laugh so much in those days, it's a shame we have lost contact with each other, but the memories will always live on in my mind.

What I can remember of my birth father he didn't do anything for me as a dad, thinking back now he never gave me cuddles or kisses, my mum did and she still does. My birth father left my mum when I was still at school, he left mum for one of her friends that she used to work with some friend huh. When my birth father left I used to go to his house for Sunday dinner, and when I got older and I starting saying to myself, here why am I sitting round here because I was getting older to realize what he had done to my mum, so one evening I phoned him up and I said look I want to see you dad but without her and he said no you see both of us or you don't see me, I said fine disown me then and I haven't heard from him since and I never want to.

My mum got married to my step dad in 1980, and they were so happy together. My step dad certainly treated my mum and I so much better than my biological father. My mum and my step dad were happily married for twenty four years and then sadly he became very ill with cancer, and that was so awful watching my dad go through that, because he was such a bubbly person he would do anything for anyone. I can remember the morning that dad had to go into hospital my mum had to take him in the car, watching dad walk out the door just in his dressing grown and slippers; it just broke my heart. I remember visiting him in hospital once when he was near the end that was so painful, he shouted at mum and I to get out of the room, it was in 2004 we lost dad. I wanted to cry so much at dad's funeral but I couldn't and I felt as if I had failed dad, but that night,

I had a picture of dad, mum and myself stuck to my wardrobe it was of when we went on the Disney Cruise Ship and we had our photo taken with the Captain, and I got into bed and I looked up at that photo and I just burst into tears, I was so very, very lucky to have a step dad who excepted me for who I am, he will always live in my memory as my loving dad to me.

My step dad took me to places where I had never been before, like Australia and that was the first time I met dads two cousins, Maureen and Jill. Maureen lived in Perth with her husband Mick, and Jill lived in Brisbane with her husband Ron, we stayed with Maureen the first week that we were out there and Maureen with her husband Mick took us to different places in Perth, and then when we went to stay with Jill and her husband Ron. They took us to the koala park that was just out of this world, and I will never ever forget when we were in Australia my step dad made my biggest dream come true, and that was to hold a koala I've always wanted to do that I even had my photo taken with the sweet koala. Which was so amazing and I even fed some kangaroo's, I was able to get right up close to the kangaroo's as well I even fed them. I will always be thankful to my step dad, my step dad treated me no different than my sisters and my brother, he used to say to me, you may be in a wheelchair but you still have a brain. Dad made me laugh, once we were on this boat trip and this woman came up to us and she said excuse me to my mum and dad, would your daughter like a sweet and my dad got so angry he looked at the woman and he said to her, my daughter might be in a wheelchair, but she has got a brain and she can talk for herself, from that moment on I knew he really cared for me as a daughter, and the first time I met dad's cousin Maureen from Australia dad introduced me as his daughter, not his step daughter I will never forget that moment. When my mum first got together with my step dad I used to call him by his name Gerry, and I said to myself, here is a lovely man who has taken me on as his daughter with my disability as well, not many men would, so I wanted to call him dad, and I think he liked me calling him dad, I know I was proud to call him my dad.

When my step dad and my mum took me to Disney Land in Florida, I met all the Disney characters like Mickey Mouse, Mini Mouse, Donald Duck, Goofy, they all came up to me and shook my hands, gave me cuddles. I remember when we went to sit down at the table for our meal on the first night on the Disney Cruise boat there was a couple sitting on our table with their children and they asked to be moved because of me and my disability, I thought to myself it was their own problem, they even had the Disney characters on the Disney boat and they came round when we were eating our meals and I had my photo taken with some of them.

I started going to a place called Strode Park, which was also for disabled people, it was in Herne Bay Kent. I went by taxi a big black one, and I had a nice driver Mick, was his name, he used to be such a good laugh. I could even take my electric wheel chair in the taxi, because it had a ramp; at Strode Park they taught me how to use a computer properly. The guy who taught computers was Brian, he was quite a laugh I used to cook there and bring what I had cooked home. Pat was the lady who taught the cooking, I got on with her as well, and there was a lady who was in charge Ross, she was my favourite for some reason, I don't know why! But I grew attached to her that's what I find though in my life I grow attached to people so easily, every so often they would review my progress of how I was getting on, they said that I was getting on well, I was allowed to keep copies of my reports. One Christmas they did a pantomime Alice in Wonderland, and we all took part, but I can't remember what part I had but and I enjoyed it, my mum came to watch.

At Strode Park I met this guy called Phil Green and we started going together, Phil was in a wheel chair himself, but he hasn't been in a wheel chair all of his life. Anyway we started going out together and the times that we had were great, one weekend I went to this place for a rest bite it was in Birchington in Kent, the place was called Crispe House. Phil was also in there at the same time as I was, and it was nice to spend more than a day with Phil, but I left Strode Park by my own accord because I was getting too close to a member of staff I couldn't let them know and I couldn't handle it. So yet again I ruined another part of my life because I let my feelings get in the way thinking back now at least I was getting out a few days a week and mixing with other people, I do regret leaving Strode Park but I have only got myself to blame.

When my two sisters got married they both asked me to be their bridesmaid, it was such an honour as they say always the bridesmaid never the bride but it doesn't bother me now I'm older, I'm just getting on with my life. I have got my mum and my mum is my best Friend in my life I owe my mum everything. She could had given me up at birth but she never did and there are times when we have our moments, and I do feel guilty when we have our rows, but I will tell you this much <u>I could not ask for a better mum</u>, I have always thought to myself, god gave me to my mum because he knew that she would had look after me so well, and he was so very right. When mum and I have bad rows she says I'm going to put you in a home, and I say go on then put me in a home, but we soon make up, I don't think I could ever live without my mum because I love her so very, very much.

In the 60's my mum used to go out working on the potato fields and my God Mother Margy Adams used to look after me for my mum, Margy lived a couple of doors down from us when we lived in Dover, I was about three or four at the time but until this very day I can remember her, she was such an evil woman. I can remember she was lifting me out of my high chair one day when she was looking after me and my foot got caught in the high chair, I screamed my head off because it hurt so much, Margy got hold of me and shut me in one of her bedrooms and when my mum came home that night and found out mum went mad at her. Mum would never let Margy look after me again, so mum started to take me with her, I can remember mum would sit me between some potato sacks to keep me sitting up straight and I used dig in the dirt for worms and I would sit there pulling all the worms apart, I was only about three or four so I didn't know any different, you wouldn't get me doing it these days.

I can remember this sweet old lady who used to live next door to us when we lived in Dover, Mrs Deadman she used look after me after school sometimes because mum had a part time job. She was so kind to me she used feed me biscuits and sweets, and she used give me drinks. Remembering my Nan, we used to go to her house every Saturday when we lived in Dover we would walk up from the town to Nan's. Well mum, my two sisters and my brother would push me of course, when we got to Nan's we always had to sit still, which was easy for me.

I think I've been so lucky in my life although I am disabled I have had such a great life and owe it all to my beautiful mum, she takes me on holiday to Spain with her every year although I do pay for myself, mum still has to look after me out there. I just want my mum and everybody out there to know that I love you mum and thank you for giving me life.

A few years back we had three pets, two dogs and one cat, they were called Joss, Scruffy and Garfield. Garfield was the cat of course, they were all my babies, when they died I cried for weeks on end, they were such loving animal's. Garfield was my cat although he used sit on my dad's lap, mum said they could sense that dad had cancer; it was around the time my dad became ill with cancer, that we lost all three of them. I keep saying to mum I want another dog like Scruffy, he was a cross between a poodle and something else, Joss was a collie cross I will always remember those sweet lovely pets of mine, Scruffy used to jump on my lap and let me cuddle him every day and Joss used to come to sit beside my wheelchair and let me stroke him.

I became an Aunty for the first time in 1980 that was when Diane had her first one. Diane has got three boys Michael, Matthew and Mark three M's, and then my other sister Lyn made me an Aunty with giving me my niece Kerry, and two nephews, which are called Jason and Stefan my brother made me an Aunty again with my two niece's Natasha, Courtney, also a nephew called Mitchell. Now I am a Great Aunty, my nephew Michael now has three children and a step son, and they are called Kalum, Kyla, Kate, and Bradley, and then my nephew Matthew has my two great niece's Amber and Lilly-Faith, and my nephew Mark has got my great niece Leah. My niece Kerry had my lovely great nephew Keion; he is so cute; my niece Kerry just made me another great aunty by having my beautiful great niece Ashleigh Louis. Then my niece Natasha had my great nephew Ty, he is so cute too and then my nephew Jason had my great nephew AAran I feel so proud to be an Aunty and a Great Aunty, but I feel so old as well.

When I was young I had to wear callipers as both my feet went over they kept my feet straight as they went over when I was a bit older I had to have an operation tendons in my legs. I was in plaster for six weeks and I had a bar between my legs. Then when the plaster came off I had to wear a cast on my legs every night when I went to bed for another six weeks, which was not very lady like. The doctors said it would help me to walk, but it didn't do any good, and then I had a second operation on my right foot to make it go straight because it went over; it didn't really make any difference I no longer needed to wear the callipers though. I didn't mind wearing them really and then as I got older they said I didn't need to wear them anymore and I could start wearing normal shoes, but these days I can only wear trainers on my feet as they are the only thing suitable for me to wear.

I get on with both of my brother-in law's Nick and Phil, Nick is married to my sister Lyn, and Phil is married to my sister Diane. Every year mum and I go on holiday to Spain with my sister Diane and my brother-in law Phil we have some good times out there. My dad's brother and sister-in law Norman and Barbra live out there, my mum and dad started going out there on their own first without me and then I started to go with them, I pay for my own air fare and save my own spending money. The place where we stay is called Coveta Fuma, when I first went out there we used to rent a villa from a lady called Sally because my dad's brother had a flat in those days, which was up a load of stairs, I remember one year my dad and my mum and my dad's brother bumped my wheel chair up the steps, you see every year Norman and

Barbra would invite us and their friends round when they had picky bits in the afternoon.

In Spain I met this lovely couple, Billy and Gloria they are English but they live in Spain, Billy is a karaoke singer out there and every year he sings to me, that song called 'Bridge Over Trouble Waters'. Billy would come and get me in my wheelchair and sit me beside him and sing to me; that would make me feel good, I even got up the courage to get up and sing. At first I used to slip out of my wheel chair because I was nervous but as the years went on I have got more confidence and even mum says my singing has got better, I think Billy gave me the confident to sing on the karaoke. Billy and Gloria have two little dogs they are called Simba and Rosie. They are such two sweet dogs I just fell in love with them straight away as soon as I saw them. Whenever I'm in Spain Billy and Gloria always brings Simba and Rosie to see me because they know I just adore them both so much. I say to Billy while I'm out in Spain Simba and Rosie are both mine, I remember one year when we were in Spain I wanted to go to a karaoke in a different bar to the place that we stay, but my brother-in law didn't want to go and I really wanted to, so Billy and Gloria said that they would take me, so I had a night out without mum. My first night out on my own since I've been going to Spain, and boy did I enjoy myself, I got up and sang on the karaoke with Billy and had a few drinks with Billy and Gloria, my favourite drink at that time and still is, is Baileys. I used to drink milk with it made it into a longer drink, and it was quite tasty but mum said, that I was putting too much on weight Baileys was quite tasty drinking it with milk, but if I want a drink of Baileys these days I have to drink it without the milk.

In Spain where we go every year for our holiday there is another lovely couple who run a bar called 'Neptuno' the couple are called Julie and Karl, and again they are so friendly. Julie's birthday is the same day as mine, but I'm a year older. I get on so well with Julie and Karl, they treat me as a normal person and that means a lot to me, and there is this guy called Mick who lives out there too, who I also became very fond of, we have been friends for years. When I first met Mick I fancied him like mad and I think Mick knew, but again we only can be friends, but hey that is better than nothing I suppose. When I go to Spain there is this dip that I really, really, love and it is called Allioli, it is a garlic dip and every time I go out there I bring a couple of pots home with me I like eating beef or chicken with it, it is really lush.

When my sisters Diane, Lyn and myself were younger my sisters took me out some Sundays to town and we would go into a café to have a cup of coffee and may be something to eat, anyway this one Sunday we were in town my sister went to put my wheel chair down the kerb and as she tipped me off the kerb as I went to pushed myself up in my chair, and then I went head first out of my wheel chair and fell onto the road, my sisters rushed to pick me up and I was ok, but then all of a sudden blood came bursting out of my fore head, there was a restraint over the road from where it happened so my sisters rushed carrying me into the restraint there were all these people eating their meals, and there was me in my sisters arms with blood pouring out of my head. I had to go to hospital in an ambulance with my sister Diane and my sister Lyn had to walk home and explain what had happened to my mum, but I don't blame my sisters for what happened at all.

When my mum was married to my biological father we used to travel up to Scotland because he came from Scotland and his family all live up there, in a place called Buckie. We used to go up by train, I remember my cousin Brenda we would always hang out together when we went up to see my uncle's and aunties, and we would always Stay at my Aunty Irene and Uncle David's house, they lived not far from the sea and the air was so fresh and the water was so soft up there. The thing I liked about going to Scotland was every morning my Aunty Irene would buy these fresh hot rolls, they were called rollies and she would put them out for breakfast, oh believe me they were just to die for I really loved eating them every morning, mum would hold one to my mouth so that I could bite a bit off, because if I had held them in my hand they would had crumbled. My Aunty Irene and Uncle David had four children, David, Brain, Brenda and Paul, I had other Uncle's and Aunties and other cousins up there and my Nan and Granddad even lived up there. Nan was so small she was only about 4ft tall I remember going to see them in their little house Nan had this little bucket of cars, and she would get them out for my brother Colin, but I would sit on the floor playing with the cars myself. I suppose you could say I was a bit of a tomboy when I was younger, as soon as my father left my mum my father's family didn't want anything to do with mum and myself also my sister Lyn my brother Colin as well, which was a shame it wasn't our fault my father left us. I remember my granddad ran a farm and he had cows on it and how it used to smell.

I have had a love for pop music since I can remember, I used to have loads of cassettes I used to sit in our front room playing and singing along. My favourite pop groups in the 70s were The Bay City Rollers, The Real Thing, Hot Chocolate and David Cassidy and there was this man and lady called Peters and Lee, the man Peter played the piano and the lady sang. I found them quite amazing because the man was blind, I also liked Abba and a few others, I think my love for listening to music comes from my teacher Mrs. Saunders, she used play the piano and the guitar.

When I was at my first school Mrs Saunders taught me how to type because I can't write by hand, so she got me a type writer I think I owe Mrs Saunders so much for being a brilliant teacher to me. Without her teaching me how to use a typewriter I don't think I would be where I am today, out of all the teachers I had throughout my school days Mrs Saunders was my very, very best.

At my secondary school we used to go horse riding every Thursday afternoon and I loved it. I used to ride a little Shetland pony called Robin, he was a lovely pony, and he was brown and white. I had to ride a Shetland pony because they couldn't lift me on a normal size horse. I enjoyed horse riding, it was riding for the disabled too, and I even got a trophy for horse riding. That was in 1979. The disabled that I went with, my friends Donna and Chris and Collette went too.

Swimming was another thing I used to do when I was at school, that was at Nonington in Kent I went every Monday evening after school with my three friends Donna, Chris and Collette, we used to have our own helpers who helped us to swim, we used to have great fun.

When I was twenty one my mum and my step dad put on a big party for me over at the community center near to where we live, mum and dad invited all my friends without me knowing it was a great night. I had a disco, I remember my friends Eddie and Barry came to my 21st and there were jelly's left over and at the end of the night Eddie and Barry came up to me and put them right in my face one each side. They were so mean to me, but they knew I could take it and then when I was forty my mum and dad gave me another big party, but this time they invited my teacher Mrs. Saunders with her husband Peter, and when I saw Mrs. Saunders there I just could not believe it, to see the teacher that I had admired so much sitting in front of me after all those years, not many people can say they had their teacher to their 40th, I'm so glad that I can.

When I have a drink I have to drink through a straw because my hands shake, I can feed myself, but I do get embarrassed because I spill some down the front of my self, so when I am out in public with mum she helps me, when I am at home I do feed myself, but when I come to the end of a meal I do need some help. Sometimes I suffer with fits so I have to take pills every day to control them I have to have three pills a day.

I still am very close to my Uncle Derek; I looked on him as an Uncle, Derek was the one who found me friends on the Internet, he sat down with me one day and we went on this web site for disable people and that's how I met my friend Karen who I call my sister, and my friend Rita they both mean a lot to me you. Also I can remember just after my dad died I was feeling down and I owe it all to Derek, so if you reading this mate a big, big thank you for taking me out in your lovely red sports car and I had always wanted a drive in his car and I thank him for that.

My dad's cousin Derek who I look on as a Uncle, helped me to find some friends on this web site for disabled people and at first I met this lovely lady Karen, she has got Cerebral Palsy too, but not as bad as mine, Karen comes from California and we have been in touch with each other for four or five years now or it maybe even longer. We are very close even though we haven't met in person, when we talk on the Internet we sometimes put our web cams on and I like that, out of all the disabled people I met on the Internet Karen is the only one who still talks to me. Then I met this man Tim, now Tim was such a laugh. Tim was in a wheel chair he only had one leg, but boy did he have a great sense of humour he used to make me laugh so much, after a while Tim didn't get in touch with me so I wrote an e-mail to him, and his dad Buster wrote an e-mail back to me saying that Tim had died. He had another stroke, I just couldn't believe it another good friend that I have lost in my life but I will never ever forget Tim and the chats that we had.

I started talking to Tim's step mum on the Internet who is Rita, now what am I going to say about my special friend Rita, well Rita as a friend means so very, very, much to me, I remember when I first talked to Rita on the Internet, she didn't realised that I was disabled. Anyway it has been a few years that Rita and I have been chatting to each other on the Internet, and we have even met each other. I have met Rita in person, she came round to see me and brought me a present for my birthday, Rita calls me her special girl, and I call Rita my special friend, I think that Rita is a very, very, special lady because she takes time out of her day every single day to talk to me, which means a lot to me we talk, we laugh and if one of us is feeling down. We are always there for each other and I want Rita to know I will always be here for her as a friend, I believe myself that Tim brought Rita into my life and for that I will be forever grateful to Tim, I just wished he was still alive though. I love my special friend Rita so very much, and I am so very proud to call her my friend, Rita doesn't like me calling her my special friend, she says to me that she is just an ordinary person who likes talking to me on the Internet, but to me she will always be my special friend because I have grown so very fond of her. I think to myself I have been so very lucky in my life for meeting friends, some friends I have lost touch with, but hey that's life isn't it, but my friendship with Rita is for life, and the same goes for my friend Karen who lives in California. Ok we haven't met each other Karen and I, but we have a special bond between us. I remember my birthday was coming up and Rita came round to see me, and we were talking on the Internet a couple of days before my birthday, and Rita asked what was my favourite cake I said I don't really have a favourite and Rita said aw come on you must have a favourite cake, so I said a coffee cake and bless her she brought me a coffee cake round and now whenever I eat a coffee cake it reminds me of my special friend Rita, I want Rita and everybody else who reads this to know that

Rita is a one in a million friend to me also I love her so very much, and I want to thank her for coming into my life and being my friend.

To be honest with you I can't believe I am where I am today, ok I can't work but I have my lap top and the Internet to some people that's nothing but to me it's my life. I first started of using a typewriter and then computers came in, my uncle Colin gave me my first computer and I am very grateful to him, and then it packed up, so dad and mum got a brand new one, but then my niece Courtney comes to us every weekend and she wanted to use the computer, so I went out and brought my first lap top and I had that for a few years and then a couple of keys came off, so I brought my self a new one and gave my niece my old one she was over the moon. My uncle Derek said to me I wouldn't be able to use a lap top, but hey look uncle Derek I'm writing this book on my lap top. I used to write poetry I don't write funny poems I like writing about people who means so much to me, to me that's how I like to get my feelings across too, I'm not very good at funny poetry but I think I do alright with the ones that I write. I love typing using my lap top, even though I can only use my left hand and one finger I think I do quite well, I am not saying I'm that good at typing, but it is something that I do enjoy writing my poems I feel I can get my feelings across more easily.

The first time that I ever went to Spain was in 1980, I went to Minorca Palma Nova I went with two of my able bodied friends who were helpers with the disabled holiday group I went with, Gillian and Heather that was the very first time I had been on a plane. I remember mum and dad took me to the airport, when I got to the airport I came out in a rash all over my chest it was my nerves, well I got on the plane alright, but as I was sitting on the plane my heart was beating so fast as we were waiting for take-off my hands went all sweaty and then came the take-off, oh boy my tummy went up into my mouth but when we were up in the air I was fine I actually enjoyed flying. When we got to Palma it was so warm I could not believe it, it was so sunny, we stayed in a posh hotel we went out every day and night. When we went out at night we went to bars we stayed out until the early hours of the morning, I remember I had my first drink of Sangria when we were there, oh I did love that drink, I drank it every single night while we were out there. There was this one night we were at a bar and that was the only drink I would drink while we were out there I got a taste for it, they brought it out to us in big jugs its red wine and a mixture of other drinks in it, I remember sitting in this bar drinking this Sangria and I looked up at the ceiling it was going round and round, but I wasn't ill. We went to the bars every night and we stayed out until the early hours in the morning, I had a great time out there and I owe all to my two friends Gillian and Heather.

I was mad on two pop stars Michael Bolton and Tony Hadley, and I have even seen them live on stage, I went to see Michael Bolton first at Wembley in London, my friend Karen who was a helper on the holidays I used to go on, she came with me. How I was able to go to see Michael Bolton was thanks to the darts team that my mum played with they all clubbed together so that I could go. I just could not believe it, I had no idea that I was going I had my own driver to drive my friend and myself up to Wembley, the only thing was wrong that all the wheelchairs were put all right at the back but it was still a brilliant night I brought my self a Michael Bolton mug, and a Michael Bolton T-shirt, I can remember my friend Karen had a bad toe that night, and we went to the ladies and as Karen lifted me onto the toilet I stepped on her bad toe, oh I did feel awful.

When I went to see Tony Hadley live in concert I went with my two friends Donna and Chris that was an awesome night, it was at the Winter Gardens in Margate Kent, we were nearer to the stage this time. I will never ever forget that night for as long as I live Tony Hadley was so good live, and then it even got better, after we saw him on stage we waited around the stage door in the freezing cold to meet Tony Hadley, and I actually got to talk to Tony I was saying to myself now stay calm and speak clearly and I did, I told Tony that him and me shared the same birthday and he looked at me and winked and said, all the best people were born on that day, I even had my photo taken with him.

When I was a young girl we had this dog called Shandy she was my very first dog, one day we were all out and Shandy was indoors by herself, and when we came back home we found that Shandy had dug a big hole in the wall, and she ripped up the carpet in the hall way after that mum got rid of Shandy, I broke my heart because I really loved Shandy I can remember when the man came to collect her I felt a big part of my life had been taken away from me then I had this lovely kitten called Blue boy he was grey and he had these lovely blue eyes, one day he had to go to the vets and my sister Lyn took him with my birth father and she was carrying Blue boy in her arms and all of sudden Blue boy bit my sister and then she let go of him and he ran off and I never saw him again, all the pets that I have had through my life I have loved so much.

I can remember my Nan, my mums mum she always used to come to ours every weekend and mum and Nan would always walk into town pushing me in my wheelchair, and when we were at home I used to sit on the floor next to my Nan playing, and now and then I would lean my head against her legs and she would stroke my hair, sadly my Nan died in 1979, I feel I was closer to mums mum than my birth father's mum even though my sister Diane was her favourite. I have got two Uncle's my mum's brother's, and they are Colin and Roy they are both special Uncle's, even though I don't get to see them, Roy is married to Ena, and Colin is married to Wendy and they are both lovely. Sometimes I do get angry for being handicapped, I am just grateful to my mum for giving me such a wonderful life. When I was younger I used to dream what it would be like to be married and have a couple of kids, but as I have got older I don't want kids of my own, to be honest I don't think that I would have the patience this is going to sound bad I loose my temper with some of my nieces and nephews, but I do love them all.

When I am indoors I use an electric wheelchair to get around indoors and when I go out I use a manual wheelchair. Once I had a friend Margaret Sharpe and she used to live round the corner from me, one day I went round to see her in my electric wheel chair and my friend had a wooden ramp going up to her front door and I went up the ramp alright knocked on the door and there was no answer so I went down the ramp again, but I went down backwards and my back wheel came off of the ramp and I banged my head, I was alright though.

To get up and down stairs at home I have got a lift that goes up through the ceiling from the living room to my bedroom and I have got two hoist one to lift in and out of bed and one in the bathroom to lift me on and off the toilet and in and out of the bath. My dream is to win the lottery and buy mum and myself a bungalow I have always wanted a bungalow.

When I was young I wore 'callipers', I didn't mind wearing them really and then as I got older they said I didn't need to wear them anymore and I could start wearing normal shoes, but these days I can only wear trainers on my feet as they are the only thing suitable for me to wear.

I have got two step brothers and one step sister and their names are Peter, Mark and Teresa. Peter has got one son called Scott, Marks got two sons called Steven and Paul, and Teresa has a son called Dan and three daughters called Nicola, Kayleigh and Tia.

In the 70s I used to go to disco's, there was one held at my school every Wednesday evening and every Sunday evening at a youth club and my brother Colin's friend Johnny Harris used to be the DJ and I used to fancy him like crazy he used to play some great music, I would take my electric wheel chair so that I could dance, I was really into my music in the 70s. Johnny came to live with us for a while because his mum and dad moved and when I was at the disco where John was a DJ I used to think I was so lucky he lived at my house.

When I wanted a ride in Uncle Derek sports car, so one day he came and took me out, I will never ever forget that, we were driving with the roof down it was so awesome. Derek has always had faith in everything I try and do. When I drink I have to drink through a stew because my hands shake, I can feed myself, but I do get embarrassed because I spill some down the front of my self, so when I am out in public with mum she helps me, when I am at home I do feed myself, but when I come to the end of a meal I need some help. Sometimes I suffer with fits so I have to take pills every day to control them I have to have three pills a day.

There was one time we was in Spain and my mum and dad and I were having a nap in the afternoon and without me knowing someone came through the bedroom window and stole my bum bag with all my Spanish money in and I had some photos of my friend Jill in there, I was more upset that I lost them than my money they also took all of my dad's money and my dad had to borrow some money from his brother Norman.

When I went to Disney Land in America on the way there we stopped off in Singapore and that was a lovely place so pretty I found it, but when we were coming back from Disney Land we stopped off in Bangkok that was such a smelly place I didn't like Bangkok at all. At Disney we went on this little ride through a cave and I could take my wheel chair on it, and as we went through the cave there were these little character's and they were all moving, it was ever so magical to see, also at Disney Land there was a safari ride, which we also went on that was awesome too, we saw a lot of animals. I could also stay in my wheelchair on that ride that's what I liked about Disney Land they catered a lot for disabled people. When we went onto coaches they lowered the steps so that I could get on in my wheelchair and sit in my wheelchair on the coach, which was good for mum and dad because they didn't have to keep lifting me in and out of my chair.

There was a time when I used to drink a lot of alcohol I used to turn to it if I felt down, but these days I can't drink a lot because I have a weak bladder and mum has to take me to the toilet, so I don't drink now only on special occasions and then I have to watch what I drink.

We moved from Dover to Ramsgate to live in the 70s, first time we moved to Ramsgate we lived in a railway house because my father worked for the railway he was a guard man, and then we moved into a council house and that the time when my mum and my birth father got divorce, so he stayed in the railway house and my mum, my middle sister Lyn, my brother Colin and I stated our new life in our new home without my father. Next door to our new house were a married couple called Ellen and John they had three girls Jackie, Susan and Melanie they were a nice family, mum and Ellen became good friends until this very day they are friends.

My step dad used to belong to a club called The Druids, and they all clubbed together to get a word processor for me, which I thought was lovely, this was before I got a computer and I used to write all my poems and all my letters on my word processor. My dad went with his brother Norman who I looked on as my uncle, and dad went with his cousin Derek who I also looked on as an uncle and I still do, sadly my dad's brother Norman died just this year it was such a shock because he was so active he used to go on walks with his wife Barbra.

I spend my days on my lap top writing e-mails to my friends or chatting to friends and family, some people would say that's a waste of time but for me it's something to do and it keeps my brain active, that's why I wanted to write this book on my life to prove to myself and other people that I can do something more with my life, and I want something to show for my life.

Just lately in my life I have learnt getting close to friends doesn't pay off but I just can't help getting close to my friends that's just the type of person I am, thinking about it now I haven't got many friends these days, I'm just so very lucky that I have got such a lovely family they have to put up with my ups and downs especially my mum bless her who I am with twenty four seven.

My mum drives our car we got it on mobility because I am disabled; we get a new car every three years. I think my mum is a pretty good driver. Mum and I go to my sister Lyn's every Tuesday and sometimes we go shopping. My sister Lyn is so good she does all the lifting with me while we are there, sometimes when we go shopping we go in a café to have a pot of tea and something to eat, and now and then I like to treat my mum and sister.

When my sister Lyn had my niece Kerry she was such a sweet little girl I just adored her and I still do, I'm not saying I don't love the rest of my nieces and nephews god knows I love them all and they have all made me very proud, but Kerry and I have always had this special bond since my sister Lyn had her. I know I said I don't like kids but as a little girl my niece Kerry was so lovely and she has now grown into a beautiful woman and I am so very, very, very proud of her. I remember when Kerry was a little girl she came to Spain with mum, dad and me, she was only about eight or nine I think and she was ever so good with us, she never moaned once while she was with us.

My eldest nephew Michael has become a lorry driver, and my other nephew Matthew is a carpenter and my other nephew Mark works in a timber yard, my niece Kerry works in a hospital and my niece Natasha works as a cleaner my nephew Jason is between jobs, and my other nephew Stefan has found it hard to find jobs because he suffers with fits, and believe me I know how frustrating that must be for him.

When I was in my teens there was a fairground in Margate, which is near Ramsgate, and the fairground was called Dreamland and there were all sorts of rides there, like a ghost train, bumper cars, and a big wheel. I used to go on all three of them, the big wheel was my favourite because you could see everything as it went round, and the bumper cars were great too, my step dad took me on the bumper cars.

There was a time in my life I went to church with a group of people, that was a time when I needed to change my life and I thought that would help me, and it did for a while but then I found that it wasn't for me, I'm not saying I don't believe I would like to think that there is something after this life but I like to keep those thoughts to myself.

My mum is a lovely cook she makes this beautiful quiche it is much better than shop ones, no one can beat my mums cooking, and mum makes these Mars Bars Rice Krispies cakes with chocolate on top they are so yummy, also my mum makes her own gypsy tart that is yummy as well.

I start my day I get out of bed by being lifting out of bed in my hoist my mum gets me out of bed and I go in the bathroom to have a shower or a wash and clean my teeth. One day I have a wash and the other day I have a shower, on the days that I have a wash I am able to wash my hands and face by myself, but when I have a shower mum has to shower me, I have to sit in the bath on a blue thing that mum has to put in the bath and pump up with a foot pump, the blue thing is meant to mould around my body to help me sit up in the bath, but it doesn't do a good job, we are meant to be getting a wet room, which should be a lot easier.

Through the day I spend most of my time just on my lap top, I have my breakfast first and while I'm eating my breakfast I like watching a chat show hosted by a guy called Jeremy Kyle who I think is so handsome, I won't move until he has finished, some of the people that go on it I think are total losers I only watch it to see Jeremy. Straight after I have watched Jeremy Kyle I go straight on my lap top and check my e-mails, some days I have e-mails from my friend Karen who lives in California we used to write to each other every day, I would write to Karen in the mornings our time and I used to get an e-mail back from Karen in the afternoon, early evening our time, which would be morning in California we have got a good friendship, we have grown that close that we call each other sisters.

I have been so very lucky with my family they have all accepted me for who I am even my niece's and nephew's, thinking about it my niece's and nephew's treat me as any other aunty, which I think is lovely and I am very, very, proud of all of my family, my three nephew's Michael, Matthew and Mark have all got their young ladies now, Michael is with Alison, Matthew is with Claire, and Mark is with his young lady Megan, and my niece Kerry has got her young man called James and my niece Natasha has got a partner called Mel, which I have no problem with at all, I must admit though when Natasha told me she wanted to bring a baby into a gay relationship at first I did have a problem with that, but I think she is a great mum just like my niece Kerry is.

Going back to my younger days my sisters and my brother were all very good I couldn't asked for better sisters and brother, to me they are the best yes we have our fights and disagreements but I'm so lucky I know they will always be there for me, and I'm so very proud of them all, and I do love them all as we have grown up I think my eldest sister Diane and I have even grown closer as we have got older, my sister Lyn and I have always been very close since we were young, my brother Colin doesn't show his feelings, but I know he cares, I think I'm so very lucky to have such wonderful sisters and brother, I just love them all.

There was a time when my sisters started going on dates and I felt a bit left out but I was just a kid and I admit I was a little bit jealous because they were going on dates and I had to stay at home. When my sister Diane was first going out with her husband Phil they used to ride motor bikes and so did my brother Colin, and they used to let me sit on them which I used to love, I used to collect pictures of motor bikes and stick them all in a scrap book by myself,

I used to enjoy doing that it was something I could do by myself.

When I was a teenager I used to like reading weekly's teenager's magazines there were three that I liked reading and they were called, Look-In and the other one was called Blue Jeans, that was my favourite because there used to be a problem page and I used to like reading the problem sometimes I could relate to, and they also had true stories I used to like reading them too. Also when I was a teenager I would have loads of posters of my favourite pop stars all over my bedroom wall. I also had this thing for Noel Edmonds, he was a DJ on the radio first in the early 70s, and he used to do a show called Swap Shop I used to watch it just to see Noel Edmonds.

The first holiday that I went on with my mum and dad was in Northampton when we stayed in a caravan, the caravan belonged to my dad's nephew, it was by this lake and there were a lot of ducks.
There and I remember I would get up every morning and sit outside the caravan and feed

bread to the ducks, that was a great holiday I enjoyed that holiday ever so much, and again I have got my mum and dad to thank for that. When my dad was alive my mum, my dad sister Diane, my brother-in-law Phil and myself all used to go out every Saturday evening to a social club called The Westgate Club they would have live bands every week, which were good. The owners were nice Sue and Dave. Sue would always come over and talked to me; mum and dad would get up and dance that was always lovely to watch, sometimes my uncle Derek and aunty Gill would come up the club too, and my brother Colin they were such good Saturday nights out, and we would come home my sister Diane and brother-in law would come back to ours and stay the night. We would sit up until the early hours of the morning chatting and laughing, I had such good days when my dad was alive I do miss him.

One year when I was going to Spain with mum and dad I was allowed to go in the cockpit of the plane with the captain as we were flying over the mountains that was amazing, the clouds looked like snow on the mountains. Every year we go to Spain the crew are very helpful with lifting me on and off the plane even when we get to Spain, they have this special chair that they lift me on and off the plane with, and when we go to get on the plane I can get on before the rest of the passengers my mum, my sister and my brother-in law can get on first with me as they are with me, I think my brother-in law Phil likes that, but when I get off the plane I have to get off last, so Phil gets off first to collect the cases, and my sister Diane stays with mum and I to help to get me of the plane. When we are in Spain my favourite place is Benidorm I just love going there it's so lively, I remember going there with mum and dad one night and I met this guy Tony was his name he was a night club bouncer and he was standing outside this night club handing out leaflets' and he looked like Michael Bolton and as we walked by he handed me a leaflet to go in the night club, and as soon as I saw him I said to mum and dad look at that guy over there don't he look like Michael Bolton and he saw me looking he came over to me and started chatting to me and then I asked him if I could have my photo done with and he agreed that made my night that did.

Every year for Christmas's and birthdays I used to make my own cards they used to be nice and then it became boring because the cards were from a disc and I just was doing the same ones over and over so I went back to buying normal cards, and the way I am able to write in them is, I brought my self a Dymo Label Writer so that it is easier for me to write in cards, the label writer slots into my lap top. When I was a young girl my mum brought me a load of toys for my birthdays and Christmas I would have a load of dolls like Cindy and she would come with all different outfits and I would enjoy dressing her up, and the other doll I had was Tippy Tumble's, I was so lucky as a little girl my mum brought me so many toys, I never went without a thing and it's all down to my beautiful mum. I think my mum is so amazing the way she has coped with me all my life, before mum met my step dad she was bringing me up on her own, words can't describe how much my mum means to me I have seen my mum go through some really hard times and I get so frustrated because all I can do is watch I feel guilty as a daughter I think I should protect her, I dread the day I will loose my mum.

I am a type of woman that doesn't like wearing dresses or skirts I used to when I was younger and then if I did wear dress's or skirt's they had to be very long, I just don't like showing my legs, and I feel more comfortable in trousers and jeans. These days I only have trousers and jeans in my wardrobe, the size of my feet I find a bit embarrassing because I am in a size two children size and I am in my 40's, even my clothes are children sizes. In the days before I owned a computer or a lap top I used to sit in my bedroom each and every night listen to my music or watch telly as I had my own telly in those days, but mum was getting worried I was spending too much time by myself. My nephew Matthew built me a desk as he is a carpenter and what a good carpenter he is; he really knows what he is doing. My nephew has a girl/friend Claire she is lovely I really get on well with Claire, my nephew Matthew and Claire have been going together for some years now, and from the first time I met Claire I knew they would be right for each other, I know I shouldn't say this, but Matthew is my favourite nephew as Kerry is my favourite niece, may be I'm wrong to have my favorites, but that doesn't mean I love the others any less, my nephew Michael is sort of quiet, I remember when Michael was young and I went to town with mum and my sister Diane, Michael was about three or four he would always have to sit on my lap, he would not walk anywhere he would always want to sit on my lap everywhere we went he used to kill my legs I think he just liked riding in my wheelchair my other nephews and nieces didn't bother about it just Michael he loved having a ride.

When my friend Jill moved to Scotland to live I was heartbroken, Jill was and still is like a second mum to me, I remember when I saw Jill before she moved to Scotland she brought me this beanie bear and I just fell in love with him, he is so soft and cuddly I take him to bed with me every night, I have named him Pookie after Garfield's bear the cartoon character, I used to collect Garfield soft toys I would have them all on a shelf in my bedroom. I had so many Garfield's and I think I have still got them, well I hope I have. I have got a love for fresh doughnuts but they have got to be fresh and hot and covered in sugar.

One year my niece Natasha and her partner Mel done a race for life for people who had cancer and I asked if I could join them because I wanted to go on it in memory of my step dad so they both took it in turns to push me in the race, and so did Natasha's mum Jayne, I quite enjoyed it even though I couldn't walk it I still took part thanks to my niece Natasha and her partner Mel and Jayne.

When I go on holiday to Spain with mum and my sister Diane and my brother-in law Phil, I go in the swimming pool near where we stay, my sister and brother-in law always helps me to get in the pool Phil gets in the pool first then my sister gets me on the edge of the pool puts me in my rubber ring because I can't swim without a rubber ring, but with my rubber ring on I'm able to swim by myself. My brother-in law Phil is very helpful while we are in Spain as there are a lot of steps Phil always bump me down and up the steps. We hire a car. There is one restaurant I love going to when we are in Spain that is this restaurant owned by this Dutch guy called Hans he is really, really nice and he does lovely food every year he sees me he always comes up to give me a kiss and a cuddle. We eat out every night while we are in Spain some nights we eat at Hans's restaurant some nights we eat the Neptuno Bar, which is owned by Julie and Karl, there is also another English couple who owns their own bar their bar it's called Sins, the couple are called Pat and Steve they are also a nice couple, they do meals, which are lovely the steaks out there are so beautiful and tender also I like my steak very rare. Mum and I share a villa with Diane and Phil they have the top half, mum and I have the bottom half, the villa belongs to Julie's mum and dad.

One time in Spain we were going back to our villa my brother-in law Phil was pushing me and we went past this dustbin. Phil stopped by the dustbin parked me beside the dustbin and walked off and left me, seeing if the bin men come soon but he did come back to get me. When I was young I used to support football teams I used support Chelsea and then I supported Southampton I only supported Southampton because Johnny Harris did, but now I can't stand football, also I liked watching snooker my favourite snooker player was Jimmy White.

My two favourite soap operas are Neighbours and Home and Away, which are Australian they are on every day they are the only two soaps I watch and really enjoy, if I'm working on my lap top I will always stop to watch them I also like to watch a soap on a Sunday mornings called Hollyoaks that's on during in the week, but it is repeated on a Sunday that's when I like watching it because I can see all the weeks worth's in one go because in the week when it's on I am normally on my lap top chatting to my friend Rita and choosing between my friend Rita or the telly my friend Rita always will come first.

Some days I get upset because I always have my dinner about five o'clock and Rita comes on line between five and seven and I don't get very long to chat to her but I treasure every second that I get to chat to my friend Rita.

When my step dad was alive he paid for the whole family to go out to Spain, with his compensation from his illness, all my sister's came with their families and my brother came with his ex-wife and all the kids came too, I remember I had a big fall out with my brother on that holiday I have been ashamed of it ever since, I never meant to start a row with my brother but it was his ex-wife that got on my nerves because she kept dumping my niece on my lap everywhere we went, and one night I had a few to drink so I said something about it but it ended up brother and I having a row then my mum slapped me around my face although apart from that night it was a good holiday, my dad fell asleep in the men's toilet and my nephew Jason was walking passed with a football, so my dad asked my nephew Jason if he could borrow the football to hide behind.

I have got this other friend when I am in Spain and that is Ian, Ian is English but he lives in Spain, I have known Ian for a few years now and we really get along, he is great to talk to, and if I loose confidence in myself he will tell me to hold my head high, just like my uncle Derek does, I have found most people have got more confidence in me than I have in myself, I am frighten that people might think I'm a show off I just want to show that I can do something in my life, and this what this book is for.

I was so glad when the Internet came in to use because I am not that good on the phone, but now I can chat to my friends and family on the Internet it has certainly change my life for the better. There are some days when I say to myself what's my life for when I have bad days like if I have had some disagreements with friends, but then again it is my fault for getting so close to people.

When I was little there were some soft toys called The Womble's there were six or seven altogether they all had different names, there was one called Wellington, I collected most of them, they had a television programme which I liked watching, when they came out in the shops my mum brought me a few of them, also I had these little toys called Weebles they used to wobble and didn't fall over I used to play with the Weebles sometimes in our back garden in a bucket of water, I used to play with my Weebles for hours and hours. I had a love for horses too in my younger days, my mum brought loads of books on horses and I loved reading about horses, I was so lucky as a child my mum didn't let me go without anything,

I can remember I had boxfuls of toys I owe a lot to my mum, mum got me a paddling pool for the back garden and that was fun, if anyone asked me did I have a good childhood I would have to say yes even though my birth father didn't have a lot to do with me with what I can remember of him, I have always thought to myself the reason he left was me he didn't want the reasonability with me.

My step sister Teresa and I get on very well when she sees me she always says 'hello sis' and comes up and gives me a cuddle, my step Sister is married to Mark who always making me laugh when I see him.

When I was young I remember going to London for day trip we went to see Buckingham Palace to see the changing of the guard and we went to London Zoo there was this gorilla and his name was Guy the gorilla, I used enjoy going up to London with my family they good times we used have picnics out. There was one time when we went to Spain on holiday and my uncle Derek and Gill his wife came, and all that holiday my uncle Derek had been cheeky to me, so on the way home on the plane I thought I would get him back as I got on the plane before Derek I sat in the first sit then when Derek came on board the plane and I put my hand out and I caught him in his private parts I did it for a laugh, that's what I love about my uncle Derek I can have a laugh with him he is a great bloke in my eyes I don't care what anyone says he is my uncle and he always will be he believes in anything I try to do. When I went to Spain the time that my uncle Derek did and I sang on the karaoke he said I used to make him laugh but he wasn't laughing at me he would never ever do that, my singing was so bad in those days even I know that, I was so nervous I used to slip out of my wheelchair.

One time in my life I tried to learn to play an electric keyboard, my mum and dad brought me one for one Christmas I really wanted to learn but I soon got bored with it, that's my trouble I get bored very easily, years ago we had a piano at home when I was young I tried to play it, I could play a bit of Amazing Grace, but only the first few notes I played it with my left hand only, but I used to enjoy trying to play the piano. In my life time I have lost so many people who meant so much to me I think to myself it's so not fair because those people who have died were so kind and so thoughtful.

With my love for music whenever I hear songs that I really like I always sing along to them, and whenever I was in the car with my Step dad, and I would start singing along to the music dad would turn the music straight off till I'd stop singing and then as soon as I had stopped singing he would turn the music on again it was so funny, I knew dad was only mucking about, and when I first sang on the karaoke in Spain they all stood up and clapped even though I knew I weren't very good.

Once my sister Lyn and my brother-in law Nick owned a caravan quite a big one it was and some Sundays Lyn and Nick would invite us over in the summer months, I used to like going over there sitting on the veranda sunbathing there was a café on the site and sometimes we would go in there to have Sunday lunch, but I would always have something different than a roast as I am not too keen on roast dinners, I used to have a cheese omelette they were nice I have a taste for omelettes especially cheese and onion ones they are so yummy. I am the type of person who loves the sun, but I burn very easily. Throughout my life I have had a lot of nicknames like, Donna doughnut because I used to like eating doughnuts, but only ones with the hole in the middle, then I got the nickname Goldfish because of the way I drank, my ex boy/friend Les named me that, and then my uncle Derek called me Twinkle, which has been my favourite of them all, I liked being called Twinkle so much by my uncle Derek that is why I have called myself it on MSN where I talk to people on the Internet.

Going back to when mum was with my birth father, I came home from school one day and found that my mum had taken an overdose, as I came home by ambulance from school the ambulance men rushed my mum to hospital to get her stomach pumped out, I will never forget that I still blame my birth father for making my mum do that to herself because that was when mum found out that he was having an affair with her friend, I will never ever, forgive my birth father for what he put my mum through. There are times when I wished I could do more things for myself, there are times when I do get frustrated with myself, but there is no way at all I feel sorry for myself for being disabled no way, in fact when I think about it if I was not disabled I would not have met all my lovely friends throughout my life, I haven't got many friends but the friends that I have got I treasure them all with all of my heart and I want them all to know this.

There was one time we were in Spain and it was the day we were coming back home to England and we had a late flight, but we had to get out of the villa at a certain time because other people were booked to have it after us, so we went and sat by the pool until it was time to go, and me being me wanted to sit right in the sun I thought that I would make the most of the sun while I can. Anyway mum kept telling me to sit in the shade, but wouldn't I listen so I ended up with a great big blister on my shoulder it hurt so much, it looked like a great big jelly sitting on my shoulder it lasted about two weeks.

When I was young I loved having long hair I had it down to my shoulders, but it did start getting matted sitting in my wheelchair all the time, so as I got older I had to shorten it, I do regret not having Long hair because I had this style with a parting in the middle and my sides flicked back that was my favourite hair style. I used to like sitting up in my bedroom in front of the mirror and brushing my hair myself while I was listening to my favourite pop music, sometimes I would sit in front of the mirror and use the hair brush as a mike and I used to sing away like mad, not that I have got a good singing voice it just made me feel good, I still sing along to my favourite songs today, but without looking in the mirror.

The way I used to get around indoors when I was young was I used sit on the floor with my legs out each side of me and I used to hop along the floor, I did find it great fun, but after I had my operation in the groin of my legs I wasn't able to, because it hurt too much so that was the end of my fun.

My mum used to work at a toy factory called 'Rovex' from nine in the morning until one o'clock in the afternoon that meant I was on my own for four hours, I was alright on my own, actually I enjoyed being on my own, in those days I was able to get to the sink in the kitchen and I used to do the washing up for mum before she got home. I admit I broke a few plates when I first started doing the washing up, but as I got a bit better, I used to do the washing up and then dry it up I didn't drop many often.

I have made another friend through the Internet, Maria is her name she comes from Spain, she is blind, I met Maria through another friend Jenny, I find Maria a kind young lady and I am so lucky that she wants me as her friend, Maria told me that she teaches blind children, and she lives by herself I really admire her for the way she copes by herself. When we were finding out about each Maria told me that her mother left her at a nunnery and she was brought up by some nuns, but now she has grown into a young independent woman, who can look after herself, she has got her own place, when I tell her that I admire her for the way she copes with her blindness she always says she is no different from me, which I suppose she is right really. Living with Cerebral Palsy doesn't bother me really, I admit there are days when I feel down and I get angry with myself because I can't do what able people do but I say to myself just think of all that I have in my life, and all the lovely people, I want to be honest my mum and my friend Rita gives me the strength that I need in my life also my uncle Derek does too, they are the important people in my life, as long as I know I have those three people I know I have everything.

I remember when my dad was alive, mum and dad would invite their friends round to our house for meals, and then they would go to their friends' houses for meals, but they would always involve me, which was nice, some Saturday night, I first had a fondue when we were in Spain it was so nice. My eating habits are so different when I go to Spain I find I have got more of an appetite, which is funny because it is so hot in Spain, but we don't eat until the evening out there. I don't like Chinese food, but we go to this Chinese restraint in Spain called Sonia's and she does this lovely chicken omelette, and she does theses beautiful prawns in batter, so when we go there my mum, my sister Diane and my brother-in law Phil all have a Chinese meal and I have my chicken omelette with my prawns in batter, it might not sound a lot, but believe me it is I think it is a lovely meal myself I must do as I eat it all. One time in Spain I was in Neptuno Bar, my uncle Norman was pushing me out of the door and instead of tipping my wheelchair backwards, my uncle Norman tipped my wheelchair forwards and I came out of my wheelchair landed on my face, I ended up with a bit of a black eye, but apart from that I was alright, I think my uncle Norman felt bad, but I don't blame him for what happened, in life you have got to expect the unexpected, when I look back it was quite funny really. My uncle Norman was my step uncle and at first he could not understand how my step dad could cope with having a disabled step daughter like me, but he always treated me so nice along with his wife Barbara, who I look on as my aunty, what I like about Barbara is since the moment I met she treated me as a normal person, I remember when we used to stay in

Norman's and Barbara had two bungalows in Spain, and I was sitting outside listening to my CD's on my personal CD player if Barbara came out and she saw me she would always lean on the wall to chat to me.

In the early eighties there used to be a pub just up the road from where we live, the pub was called 'The Flowing Bowl', mum, dad and I went up there now and again they used to have a disco some nights, I remember there was this barman who I had my eye on, Peter was his name, I remember this one night we were up there and there was a disco on and I asked for a request to be played to Peter from me. The song I asked to be played was called You'll Never Walk Alone, when the DJ put the record on he said this is dedicated to Peter from Donna, and Peter walked from behind the bar to come to stand beside me while that record was playing, Peter really made my night that night.

My sister Lyn used to work in a hairdressers in Ramsgate called 'Diane's' and mum used to shampoo the lady's hair and I had to go with her in case I needed the toilet, there was a lady who came to the hairdressers, Mary was her name she came in every Saturday mornings my sister Lyn did her hair, and she would always make a point to come and talk to me, it was my birthday on a Saturday one year and Mary came in as usual to have her hair done, she came up to me and she handed me some beautiful flowers in a basket it was so nice of her, I don't get to see Mary anymore but she will always stay in my memory as my friend.

Once we were on holiday in Spain we went to see some dolphins and it was out of this world, it was so awesome watching the dolphin's doing all their tricks, I think they are such cleaver animals, when I was watching the dolphins I got so emotional they really touched my heart, to get to the dolphins there was a steep hill and thanks to my brother in law Phil, and my nephew Matthew they both took it in turns to push my wheelchair up the hill, which I was very grateful for. I will always remember going to see the dolphins that will also be the one thing that will live in my mind that my mum and dad took me to see, thanks to my mum and my dad I have got some great memories.

Through my life I have many people who I have become friends with and I am very, very lucky, but in my eyes I have got two very special Friends that no other ones can ever compare to them, and they are Jill and Rita they have shown me what real friendships are thanks to? Them I know that I will always have two very dear friends in my life, let me tell you about Jill first, although I have wrote about our friendship a few lines back I wanted to write some more, after Jill moved up to Scotland I thought that I would never be able to see her ever again, but it was my birthday it was a Saturday mid-morning and the doorbell went my dad went to open the door and this lady stood in front of him, my dad didn't recognize her she said hello I have come to see Donna, well when I saw Jill standing there in my home I just could not believe my eyes, Jill really made my birthday that year she brought me a fleece a light blue one, which I loved, but the best present that she gave to me that year was by surprising me with a visit, I got mum to take my photo with Jill, which was lovely but sadly I have not got that photo anymore as it was in my bum bag when it was stolen on holiday I was so upset over that as that was my favourite photo of Jill and I, although I have another photo of Jill and I with Jill's grandson Clark when we went to London Zoo. That photo sits on my desk where I sit on my lap top all day, I will always have a special place in my heart for my friend Jill, and as for my other friend Rita she gives me comfort when I need it I have been bless by these two friendships, my friendship with Rita was so easy making friends with she makes me feel comfortable like my disability isn't there and she sees me for who I am, the conversations we have on the Internet. Sometimes I forget that I am disabled, Rita sends me photos of her family and I really do enjoy getting them from her, I have got a special folder for all Rita's photos, I have so many, I just love receiving photos of Rita with her of Rita and her family which I love and treasure each and every one of Rita's photos, I just feel so lucky to have best friends like Jill and Rita in my life, as I know I have got my beautiful mum as well I know I have got all the love that I ever need in my life.

Remembering the times and the days out that I had with my friend Jill they were just amazing times, she took me to France just the two of us Jill phoned my mum up and said could I borrow your daughter to take on the boat, so we went to France for the day, Jill took me all on her own, now is that a good friendship or what, well Jill your friendship means so much to me, not many able bodied people have taken me out like that, but my friend Jill did and I thank her from the bottom of my heart, to me Jill is a second mum to me she said to me that she thinks it is an honor that I think of her as my second mum, but it does not mean I love my mum any less no way.

I like to spend my evenings sitting listening to the local radio while being on my lap top, but at the weekends I can't listen to my music because my brother Colin sits in the kitchen on his lap top and he has the television on, so there is no point in having my music on, through the weeks nights I love it because I have my dinner about five or just after, and I am straight back on my lap top until my bed time, which is at eleven o'clock.

Because my mum has to wash me when I am in the bath they suggested putting a wet room in what a lot of work went into that, one man came to pull the bath and toilet out, his name was Steve he was such a nice guy I could not believe they sent just one workman on his own, they said it would take just under two weeks yet it took just over two weeks, so for those two weeks mum had to give me stripped washes, I could not have my hair washed which was awful because I love my hair washed. Then when I could finally use it there were some setbacks to it the chair that they supplied for me to sit under the shower also over the toilet was no good at all, the wet room it's self is great it's the seat that they supplied me with, I started using the shower the first day that went alright but the second day I used the seat something awful happened as mum was wheeling me in the seat back into my bedroom my body went sideways and my leg got caught as it slipped through the gap in front of the seat, as mum was trying to get me out the more my leg got caught. I ended up with a bruise on the top of my leg, the day that it happened luckily my brother Colin was off work sick with a bad shoulder he had to come to help mum, after then he kept making jokes about seeing my bottom, the shower chair is so big it is such hard work for mum bless her. Something they said would make it easier is so much harder especially for mum, but when they were doing the wet room they supplied me with a commode to use, when they were putting the new toilet in, but when it was all finished the toilet wasn't suitable for me to used, so we asked the man who brought the commode with him if we could keep it and he said yes they only throw them away after, so it stays in my bedroom as I have still got a hoist in there, but my poor niece Courtney can't sleep in my room anymore because I have my electric wheelchair in my room on charge overnight, then there is my commode chair so for now she has to sleep on the sofa. I want to tell you a bit about my wonderful mum and why I think she is so wonderful and so amazing, my mum has basically brought me up by herself, she is not only my mum she is my best friend in my life, yes we do have our disagreements sometimes but I know that I am so very lucky to have a mum who is so patient with me, without my mum I don't think I would be where I am today, what I am trying to say is there is no other mum like my mum, she puts everybody else first before herself, I do worry about my mum copping with me as we both get older, but she keeps going bless her heart.

Even though I was born with cerebral palsy I have had such an incredible life thanks to my mum and my step dad, god bless him also my two sisters Diane and Lyn, not forgetting my brother Colin, I could not asked for a better family, when I sit and think about it I have the best family in the world, and being cerebral palsy is nothing really, there are many people worst off than me in this world, also the friends that I have made in my life mean so much to me too.

My friend Maria who lives in Spain and we are that close that we call each other sisters, Maria has been teaching me Spanish while we are chatting she has taught me quite a lot of Spanish words like, 'Te Quiero' which means I love you and also 'Angel mio' which means Angel sister, she has taught me much more, I find it so enjoyable Maria is so patient with me. So this is my life so far I am living in spite of cerebral palsy, which sometimes is not easy for my mum to cope with me, so I would like to dedicate this book to my beautiful mum who has always been there through the ups and downs and also I would like to dedicate this book to my mum who dedicated her life to looking after me, and to my step dad who took me on as his own daughter

I would like to write about these lovely couple David and Joanna Barnes, I first started chatting to David on a disabled website called Ablehere. I found I got on so well with David straight away we just clicked the very first time we started chatting, I remember David wanted to take mum and I out for fish and chips, but mum said no, I felt so sad because I so wanted to meet David and Jo, anyway I kept chatting to David and our friendship started to grow, and then we started to chat on MSN Messenger every day. David is the kindness man that I have ever known, he makes me laugh whenever I feel sad and he makes me feel special although I think I'm not, he is always telling me that I am, he even calls me his Special Sweetheart and I call David my Special Sunshine because he is always brightening my days up. Christmas of 2011 David and Jo wanted to come and see me and at last mum let me meet them both; that just made my Christmas. I was just worried that David and Jo would not be able to understand, but we started talking and to my amazement they understood me, I was so glad I just wished I could see more of David and Jo on a regular base's because they mean the world to me and I am so very glad that they came into my life. David and Jo I can't put into words what you both mean to me.

My sister Lyn and brother-in law Nick I would like to write about them now, near the end of 2011 they moved from Dover to Ramsgate and at this time my mum was in a lot of pain with her shoulder, so when my sister and brother-in law got settled into their new house. One Sunday in 2012, mum was in so much pain as she was getting me up and showering and getting me dressed, she came down stairs she could hardly walk she was in that much pain. So my brother Colin went to see my middle sister Lynn who had just moved from Dover to Ramsgate, and Colin said to Lynn mum was finding it hard to see to me, so my sister offered to come and get me up each and every morning, Lynn gets me up and showers me and get me dressed each and every morning. In my bedroom I have got a radio and every morning Lynn puts it on we both like listening to the local radio called Academy FM, and every morning while Lynn is getting me dressed we both listen to it, and there is this quiz called 'The Test Of Ten' and while Lynn is getting me dressed we try to answer them, but I am not very good, I get some right, but Lynn is pretty good she always makes me laugh when she gets a question right she is always thrilled when she gets a questions right. We have our off days with each other just like any other sisters, but what my sister does for me I just think she is the best sister in the world.

In 2013 I became 50 and that is where I conclude my life story for now, I would like to dedicate this book to my mother Valerie Hughes and my father Gerald Hughes who are in my eyes such loving wonderful parents, and I love them both ever so very much with all my heart.

By Miss Donna Hughes

Printed in Great Britain
by Amazon